PSYCHO IMAGINATIONS

PRABH JOT SINGH

ISBN 979-888555735-1

Contents

Preface

When I was a kid I used to hate my life for no reason, at that time I just created one more small me through my imagination....I use to talk to him & say him I wanna die, I attempted many suicides but was fail to do so......And then I discovered I am different from all the people in this world.....I am here to do something that no one can do....I meditated for a long time and discovered the inner me.......

CHAPTER ONE

Self Psycho Matters

You can do what you think you want to do.

God told us not to replace old environment with the upcoming modern techniques. Old things don't change by new thinking.

The "subconscious mind" is not a mind but a goal revolving mechanism around brain & nervous system, used and directed by the mind.

Humans does not have two minds, it has only one consciousness that operates an neutral automatic goal, which can be either a victory or a failure.

CHAPTER TWO

Arouse The Success Within You

For getting successful: Take conscious mind decision, get imagination of the goals.

Sunlight, scatter is gentle. Focus on the imagination, don't be aimless. Stay always focused, it can help you improve self-image and automatic success mechanism to reach goals.

"Timonel" from Spanish word meaning "the steersman."own mechanisms steer their way to a goal, target, answer.

Science can build the computer but not the operator.

There are two types of self mechanisms: where you don't know your goal and you have to still find it, or you know your goal and you are about to achieve it.

When you want a new idea or an answer for a question, you should believe that the answer already exists in yourself.

CHAPTER THREE

Imagination The Valuable Key To Your Preprogram Success Apparatus

Your nervous system can't tell the difference between an imagined experience and a real one.

People gets hypnotized by their self-images.

The brain that reacts to the environment is the same brain that tells us what the environment is.

So if our psychogenic pictures about ourselves are senseless, our reactions towards the environment will be undignified.

Mental practice is as powerful as real practice.

Imagine a movie in which you are playing different roles in various situations.

CHAPTER FOUR

Get Out Of Flawed Beliefs That Dehypnotize You

The difference between psycho and imagination is— in psycho we imagine the most powerful things whereas in imagination we achieve them. Both includes fantasy, external, superficial, unrealistic.

Belief is power of the power of hypnosis.

It doesn't matter at all from where you just imagine the things but if you do then you have the power to achieve it.

Within you is the ability and power to do whatever you need to do to be happy and successful, do things you never dreamed possible.

Just come out of yourself from "I can't," "I'm not worthy," "I don't justify it".

CHAPTER FIVE

Succeed With The Power Of Astute Envision

Your automatic mind works on the data you give it in the form of recommendation, faith and opinions.

Astute Envision — Conscious mind decision, imagination which communicates to target instructions to the self implement.

All skill learning is accomplished by trial and error. Negative experiences don't discourage, but contribute to the learning process.

But once an blunder is recognized, it must be consciously out of mind, and the victorious attempt dwelt on.

CHAPTER SIX

Calm And Let Your Self Mechanism Be Activate

Our problem is: we ignore our push button creative mechanism and try to solve all problems by conscious willpower.

Awake mind: poses and IDs problems, but not solve them. That causes stress.

You can't even pick up a pencil by conscious thought.

Depending on conscious thought and willpower = careful, anxious, fearful.

How to Think Like Prabh Jot Singh: genius is a process, not gift.

CHAPTER SEVEN

Procure The Addiction Of Cheerfulness

Cheerfulness is neither earned nor deserved, but a simple state of mind. It is a natural accompaniment to the being and acting.

Life is a series of complication. If you want to be cheerful, be cheerful.

A dominant cause of depression is taking things personally that are not personal at all.

Cheerfulness is a mental frame of mind in the present, not future.

Cheerfulness is a symptom of normal functioning. Mankind functions when they're reaching for victory.

CHAPTER EIGHT

Component Of The Success Type Personality

One of the best ways of helping people have a fortunate personality.

Some people have never develop a good image of themselves in a new role, so being in that role upset them.

Get a goal worth working for & always have a project to look forward.

The success-type personality is made of:

Sense of direction: don't think of what others expect, but think about what you want.

Understanding: depends on good connections with people. Most failures in human relations is misunderstandings.

Courage: best shield is strong felony, have courage to bet on yourself.

Charity: wealthy individual realize each person is a child of God. If you don't feel that people are very important, you can't respect yourself deep down.

CHAPTER NINE

Evade Mistakenly Activating Your Preprogrammed Failure Mechanism

Bad signals to FAILURE:

Frustration

Aggressiveness (misdirected)

Insecurity

Loneliness

All of these developed as solutions to problems.

Frustration: If you're constantly frustrated, either your goals are unrealistic or your self image is insufficient, or both.

Aggressiveness, misdirected: aggressiveness follows unchecked frustration. Aggressiveness is necessary to reach a goal. It's not abnormal. But misdirected, it's dangerous.

Insecurity: Sign of loosing trust from family,friends,relations,etc. A insecure man can never achieve anything in his career.

Loneliness: a worst situation of being alone but wanted to connect with people. Human Beings are the most lonely creatures in this universe, when a individual is lonely they are also not satisfied with human contact.

CHAPTER TEN

Eliminate Sentimental Marks And Give Yourself An Sentimental Face Lift

Physical body forms a callus to prevent re injury to the same spot, we do the same with sentimental injury, becoming hard hardhearted and callous.

Spiritual mark tissue protects human only from the human who really hurt them, but also all other human beings.

Humans avoid the situation from where they know they can get hurt. They also stop listening to there heart voice, what it wants.

Alone people also feel out of touch with their real self and life.

CHAPTER ELEVEN

Unseal Your Original Character

"Character" is the evidence of the unique creative self made image in front of God.

The original self in every individual is attractive, has a powerful impact and guidance on others.

Search chances and surroundings where you can operate without fear or inhibition to prove your competence to your self image.

"Scopo tremore" when your hand shakes just as you are about to thread a needle.

You get more negative feedback & poor performance when you are too concerned of what others think.

CHAPTER TWELVE

Sedative That Calms Mind

Most of the people don't need drugs. You already have sedatives you can use.

If a mobile rings, you might answer it out of habit. But you don't have to. You can form a new habit of not replying.

There are a lot of disturbing noises in our environments to which we've become conditioned.

You can meditate on regular basis it will calm you and increase your strength towards controlling your anger.

Develop your own personal great hot routine with a good coffee & a peaceful area.

CHAPTER THIRTEEN

How to Turn a Crisis Into a Creative Opportunity

Make a habit to expertise skills without compulsion.

React aggressively, not defensively, responding to the challenge not the menace.

Analyse the crisis from a true perspective.

Not tense, but “spirited.” Same as race horses.

Excitement can make people stumble or perform better than ever.

You don’t want your life to become a soap opera where everything is a crisis.

Change panic to: “I have everything to gain and nothing to lose”.

CHAPTER FOURTEEN

GRAB & KEEP "THAT SUCCESSFUL DESIRE"

Our mind is goal oriented, if its not used it get lazy.

Call up the desire of success, and you will act lucky. When you experience the "winning feeling" your internal is set for success.

When we remember, neurons discharge an electric current. A pattern of neurons form a chain in the brain tissue you just furnish the spark to bring that action pattern to life.

Feeling something and taking action on it or imagined feelings and then taking action are both circular process.

Try for small goals to get success winning feeling. Start with easiest where you know you will win.

Success builds on success. Fast Track success in the theater of the Mind.

CHAPTER FIFTEEN

THE LONG YEARS OF LONG LIFE NO LIMITS

Our body is designed to heal itself from various stress.

Snake usually don't stress, and healing is usually consistent in them.

Humans who heal faster are optimistic and have something to look forward to.

Evolve a remembrance for the future instead of the past.

Medical feeling and faith derive from the same source and should work together.

Humans are the only creatures which are evolved so much from the past centuries so they should live stress free as long as they are alive.

About The Author

PRABH JOT SINGH

For more information about forthcoming titles in this series, Follow me on Social Media.

Consider leaving a review of this book to help other readers!

Both positive and negative reviews are greatly appreciated.

Enjoyed this book? Share it with a friend!
You can connect with me on links given below or scan qr code:

https://linktr.ee/prabhjotsinghofficial
http://www.facebook.com/prabhjotsinghofficial
http://instagram.com/prabhjotsinghofficial

SCAN QR CODE TO CONNECT WITH ME !

9 798885 557351

Printed by Libri Plureos GmbH in Hamburg, Germany